BIRDING
NANTUCKE

MW00466197

Kenneth Turner Blackshaw (signature)

By Andrews and Blackshaw

(Edith Folger Andrews
and
Kenneth Turner Blackshaw)

Illustrations by George C. West

Copyright © 2014 by Edith F. Andrews and Kenneth Turner Blackshaw

All rights reserved. No part of this publication may be reproduced or transmitted in any form or by any means, electronic or mechanical, including photocopy, recording, or any information storage or retrieval system, without permission in writing from the authors.

Library of Congress Cataloging in Publication Data

Andrews, Edith F., and Blackshaw, Kenneth T.

    Birding Nantucket

ISBN – 1-4196-6625-8

Manufactured in the USA

EX LIBRIS

Table of Contents

Sanderlings

Introduction

  Birding Nantucket, now in its eighth edition, is 37 years old and has been a joyous collaboration between these two authors.

  With each update, we refine the bar graphs to better reflect current conditions and hone the text to better reflect new bird trends and habitat disruption by increased development pressure on our fragile island.

  This book is aimed at the study of the birds of Nantucket Island. The vast majority of the information provided is applicable to the type of trip that may be easily taken in a single day from the town of Nantucket using a car or bicycle. A new addition at the end of the text describes a wonderful series of bird walks you can take on the island.

  This book is intended as a companion to a field guide you are probably already carrying. For suggestions, check out the Selected References at the end of this book. Our guide's purpose is to show you what birds are here in which season, and where to find them. The identification is up to you!

  The format for this guide was inspired by *A Field List of Birds of the District of Columbia Region*, a publication of the Audubon Naturalist Society of the Central Atlantic States. We thank them for their permission to utilize many of their ideas.

  The first section of ***Birding Nantucket*** is a seasonally organized description of various trips you can take to island birding locales and the birds you might find. We tell you how to bird the island at any time of the year.

  We realize that most birding is done in the summer months. Those of you who visit Nantucket during other seasons will find birding even more enjoyable (with the possible exception of the dead of winter). Spring and fall migrations bring us a continuously changing population of birds, ranging from loons through longspurs. Also in the off-season one finds fewer people around and the birds are often easier to approach.

The bar charts provide the most up-to-date information available on the distribution and seasonal variations of the island's avifauna. There is an additional list covering those species considered accidental (those with five or fewer records over the past fifty years). The status of each bird is meant to indicate its frequency of occurrence in its most usual habitat. Remember, every year is different – one of the joys of birding. These bar charts have now been revised many times and with each revision we agonize about the thickness and extent of the bars.

The habitat map covers all significant habitat categories found on the island. The categories may be used with the data given elsewhere in the book, especially the map, in order to locate likely areas to find a particular species.

If you see a bird that is not on the list, or one that is outside the normal seasonal variation patterns we have delineated, please report all details of the situation to:

Mrs. Edith F. Andrews   Mr. Kenneth T. Blackshaw
P.O. Box 1182   or   4 Sandwich Road
Nantucket, Mass. 02554   Nantucket, Mass. 02554

In this day and age, e-mail is often a more efficient tool to use. Contact Edith at efa@nantucket.net, or Ken at curlewbird@comcast.net. Also, you may want to check out the 'Birding Nantucket' Facebook page.

We are anxious to be able to add to our knowledge of the island's birds and recognize that in many ways, a book like this only scratches the surface. Our aim is to provide a tool for any birder at any level of expertise who has a chance to sample Nantucket's bird life. The more people who can study our birds, the more we shall learn about them.

One final note, if you are thinking about driving on Nantucket's beaches, be sure that your vehicle has the proper permit sticker to do so. Also there are certain areas that are restricted due to private property, erosion, and/or the nesting of species that are threatened (Piping Plover and Least Tern).

Good luck and good birding.

The Authors

Seasonal Birding on Nantucket

Like most other areas in the Northeast, Nantucket has a different bird population in each season. The following pages describe the best ways to find Nantucket's interesting bird species in any season. Use the map in the center of the book in conjunction with these descriptions. It's a good idea to start with winter and read through the other seasons because you'll need to refer back to the directions in order to find some of the good birding areas. Who knows – what you read under "winter" may bring you back for another visit.

Remember, the prevailing sunlight pattern will give you better observing conditions if you bird the west end of the island in the morning, and the east end in the afternoon. Also, visiting a spot at the time of high tide is often very different from when it is low. Check the times in the newspaper or on the radio since they change every day.

Purple Sandpiper

Winter Birding on Nantucket

A good short trip in winter and also in spring and fall is to take Cliff Road out of town to check Maxcy's, Washing, and Capaum Ponds (1). You can get to Cliff Road by starting near the Whaling Museum and going north on North Water Street. You bounce along the cobbles for a while but will eventually cross Easton Street and then bear slightly left as you head up Cliff Road. Set your odometer to zero as you cross Easton Street and proceed 1.4 miles to where you reach Tuppancy Links on your right. This old golf course is owned by the Nantucket Conservation Foundation. It's a wonderful place to walk if you have some time, particularly if you like the company of dog lovers. But you might want to save it for when it is warmer since the area is quite exposed to the wind.

Continuing to drive on Cliff Road, it's another 0.3 miles to the junction of Washing Pond Road. Turn right here and follow this road 0.4 miles to where you see a concrete Public Way marker beside a rutted road through some pines. This pine grove often harbors some interesting land birds. Just a little farther along brings you to a parking area. Be careful of the soft sand on the edges. You can park here and look over Capaum Pond, the site of Sherburne, the first Nantucket settlement before the barrier beach to your right closed off the little harbor in 1700. The light is good from this vantage point in the early morning and you should easily find Red-breasted and Hooded Mergansers, both species of Scaup, Ring-necked Ducks, and many Buffleheads along with the Herring Gulls that seem to love to come to this spot to bathe. It's also possible to walk over to the top of the dune to the north and find loons and eider that may be feeding along the edge of Nantucket Sound.

Drive back out to Cliff Road and turn right for just about 0.1 miles. Here Charnes Way starts out as paved, and then crosses the bike path. From this spot you can see Maxcy's Pond to your left and also visit Washing Pond (where they used to wash out the sheep wool) on your right. You can actually drive down the rutted road and park near Washing Pond, but you may have better luck parking near Cliff Road and walking in. That way, you may find a hardy winter catbird or perhaps an Orange-crowned Warbler with the hoards of Yellow-rumps that inhabit that area. Washing Pond supports the same species of ducks that you found in Capaum. You may find Ring-necked Ducks there (and in Maxcy's) as well. If you

8

are birding later in the day, the light will be better for viewing the birds over in Maxcy's. There is a little path that leads down from the rudimentary parking lot that affords a good view from the pond's edge, looking south.

About 0.3 miles farther out Cliff Road you will find Capaum Pond Road winding up the hill to your right. Turn here and proceed toward the shore past the frantic construction of too large houses. At the high point there is an excellent view of Capaum Pond from the west, a really good afternoon vantage point. This road continues along as you bear to the left, and comes out on the Eel Point Road less than 1.0 mile later.

If you have more time to bird, start your next trip by continuing out Cliff Road to where it joins the Madaket Road. Else, reverse your direction to town for a warm cup of quahog chowder.

A longer trip in winter is to take the Madaket Road out of town to the North head of Long Pond. As you travel west on Main Street, set your odometer to zero as you pass Caton Circle and start out the Madaket Road. It is 1.6 miles to the parking lot for the Sanford property that is a Nantucket Conservation Foundation

Long-tailed
Ducks

sanctuary. This provides good walking access to several other ponds including the North Head of the Hummocks and the west side of Hummock Pond. If it's a fine day, it is a three-mile walk to the beach. You will cross territory frequented by Northern Harriers and sometimes, Northern Shrikes. Keep an eye out for American Tree Sparrows. At one time, Short-eared Owls could be found in the sand-plain grassland habitat closer to the ocean.

If you choose to drive on toward Madaket you will pass the junction with Cliff Road in 0.2 miles. This is the connection point from the first winter trip. Long Pond is several miles farther along the Madaket Road.

Once you reach Long Pond (2), there is adequate parking on both sides of the road at 'First Bridge.' If you want to bird from the car, you can park on the right-hand side where you can get a full view of the North Head. Here you can expect to see Redheads (this is one of the best areas in the state to see Redheads), Greater and Lesser Scaup, Ring-necked Ducks, Canvasbacks, Buffleheads, Hooded and Common Mergansers, Pied-billed Grebes, American Coots, American Wigeon, and with luck, a Eurasian Wigeon. You may be fortunate enough to find some Gadwalls and a Ruddy Duck. Be sure to check out the swans. The Mute Swan flock grows to 150 during the winter and sometimes a few Tundra Swans will show up with them. Occasionally the North Head fills with Herring and Great Black-backed Gulls displaced from the nearby landfill. Take a look at what's on the south side of the road as well.

Back in your car, you can proceed west to the top of the rise where you will find a road with a sign for Warren's Landing branching off to the right. The road is paved for the first six 0.6 miles. 0.2 miles beyond that, you come to a public way marker that shows where to turn for a parking area providing an excellent view of Madaket Harbor.

At low tide, many bars are exposed that may be good shorebird resting-places. A spotting scope is required to see most of these. Here you should find Long-tailed Ducks, Common Goldeneyes, Bonaparte's and Ring-billed Gulls, along with the hordes of Herring and Great Black-backed Gulls. If you look toward Eel Point to the north, you may pick out some Brant and also Great Cormorants.

Go back to the main Warren's Landing Road and continue another 0.3 miles where you can park looking out over the Eel Point dunes. On the way, you will go through a grove of pines that harbors winter finches in years when they are present. Don't go beyond the 'soft sand' sign unless you have 4-wheel drive and a Beach Permit. There is a wide spot in the road where there is room to park several cars (4). If you don't have four-wheel drive, you will have to leave your car and walk. You can go north to the shore of Nantucket Sound. Here at low tide you will see a number of sandy shoals that may be covered with Herring and Great Black-backed Gulls, Black-bellied Plovers, and flocks of Sanderlings. Harbor and Gray Seals haul out on these shoals, sometimes by the hundreds.

If you do have four-wheel drive and a Beach Permit, you can drive out to the beach and then turn left (west) and drive about a 0.25 miles to a point where there is a great view of a tidal bay known as the "bathtub." This is often full of seasonal shorebirds and waterfowl. This is also where a rare Little Egret has been observed during several summer seasons.

There are other roads in this area that allow you to reach the "bathtub" area from the south. The sand dunes in this area are an excellent place to look for the Ipswich race of the Savannah Sparrow. Although it's not currently recognized as a species, it may be in future revisions. You may also flush some Horned Larks. About half the winters produce a Snowy Owl somewhere in this area.

If you don't mind some large potholes, you can continue along the Eel Point Road as it curves back around toward Dionis. In years past, this was a good spot for Short-eared Owls. They may be back in the future. This road eventually connects with the Madaket Road.

We'll assume you have returned to the intersection of Warren's Landing Road and the Madaket Road. 0.2 miles farther along will bring you to Second Bridge that is another good area for duck viewing. Even in extremely cold weather, this section will have open water giving you an opportunity for some of Nantucket's unique waterfowl like Redheads. Certainly Mallards will be begging for food. The little parking lot there gives you another vantage point from which to view the pond as well as a look at the brackish marsh around Hither Creek to the west.

We now describe a side-trip here that will lead you over an area called the Head of the Plains. If it is getting toward sunset though, we'd suggest skipping this section and picking up a few paragraphs farther on where the far west end of the Madaket Road is described.

Just a few tenths of a mile beyond Second Bridge, bear left on a diagonal road, Long Pond Drive. This road dead-ends on a dirt road known as South Cambridge Street. Turn left here and you will quickly come to a short wooden bridge across another neck of Long Pond, Massasoit Bridge. This is another excellent spot to see Black-crowned Night-Herons and other marsh birds. Virginia Rail has been seen here. There is a spring that enters the pond just to the east and this section will often be open even though most of the pond is frozen. Wigeon, Ring-necked Ducks, Hooded Mergansers, and perhaps a Gadwall may be seen here.

Continue straight across the bridge and bear slightly to the right and you are on Red Barn Road. This road will eventually parallel the beach. Keep in mind that erosion conditions may bring the beach and the road to the same point, so use caution.

After a mile or so you will reach a point where the road bends to the left overlooking a large body of water known as Clark's Cove. This is a wonderful afternoon lookout point for many species of waterfowl. Beginning in early April you may also see some spectacular Osprey activity around the nesting pole that is visible from here, over in Ram Pasture (24).

If you have a four-wheel drive vehicle with high clearance, you may continue north here along the west shore of Clark Cove for more waterfowl vantage points. This road passes through some excellent Northern Shrike and harrier habitat, eventually joining Barrett Farm Road and ending back on the Madaket Road.

Great Blue Heron

Start reading here if is later in the day and you are thinking about the Long-tailed Duck flight. If you have time, continue on the Madaket Road all the way to the ocean (5). Here is a good spot to observe both loons and gannets. If you're there from 3 p.m. to sunset you may see flocks of Long-tailed Ducks, often numbering

12

in the hundreds of thousands, flying west in a steady stream. At times these flocks are close to shore. Sometimes they are far enough out that you will require a spotting scope. The ducks may cut across the Smith's Point opening or fly over Tuckernuck to reach Nantucket Sound where they will spend the night. In the early morning, the flight is reversed with the flocks leaving the Sound and heading for the open ocean.

Look for Ames Avenue that will take you across Millie's Bridge towards Smith's Point. Drive slowly through the pine grove as often this will produce interesting flocks of winter finches, or at the least, Yellow-rumped Warblers.

Be careful not to drive in the soft sand at the end of the road. At any time of day, take a look over Madaket Harbor from Jackson Point (25), for diving ducks and cormorants.

Yellow-rumped Warblers

An alternate trip would be the exploration of the east end of the island by taking the Milestone Road toward Siasconset.

You will eventually reach 'Sconset Village. From the flagpole at the center, bear right to Gully Road that runs downhill to the beach, passing under a wooden walkway. This area is known as Codfish Park (6).

Park in the little lot that faces the beach and check out the grove of pines nearby. This is a great haunt for sparrows, chickadees, and nuthatches, not to mention flocks of Yellow-rumped Warblers. You might even find an Orange-crowned Warbler here.

Check out the ocean for Northern Gannets fishing Pochic Rip, Common and Red-throated Loons, Horned and Red-necked Grebes, all three scoters, Great Black-backed Gulls, Common Eiders, Razorbills, Common Murres, Dovekies and, with on-shore wind, there may be thousands of Herring and Bonaparte's Gulls. This beach is one of the best places in New England for Iceland and Lesser Black-backed Gulls. Scan the flocks of Bonaparte's Gulls carefully for the black underwings of a Little Gull.

Every year is different. When Bonaparte's Gulls are abundant, Black-headed and Little Gulls may also be present. Note: There are several vantage points along the south shore where pelagics may be observed, from the old Naval Facility near Tom Never's Head, to Cisco (pelagic lookouts are marked with a (P) on the Location Map).

Still in Codfish Park, drive to the north end where there is a brushy area below the bank. It is worthwhile stopping here to listen and perhaps try and call birds in. A late winter Yellow-breasted Chat is possible. In spring, Blue Grosbeak has been found here.

Return to the flagpole and take the first right and then watch for the last left that is Front Street. The first paved road to the right is Butterfly Lane (about 0.4 miles) that ends on Baxter Road. Travel due north to Sankaty Head Lighthouse (7). Here you used to be able to park and walk to the bluff and have a full view of the ocean. Now beach erosion has made that impossible. The best you might do in the winter is look for access points from which you can view the ocean as you approach the lighthouse. Looking toward the horizon with a spotting scope, it's sometimes possible to see thousands of scoters, Long-tailed Ducks, and eiders. From December to March you should be able to add Harlequin Ducks here, and with luck, a King Eider.

Return to the Polpis road via Bayberry Lane and follow it toward Sesachacha Pond. Watch for the concrete post marking Hoick's Hollow on the right (about half a mile). This road leads you to an ocean overlook adjacent to the 'Sconset Beach Club. If there is water in the big puddle where the road dips, check this for drinkers and bathers. Yellow-breasted Chat has been seen here in early winter. This ocean overlook is good for scoters, Long-tailed Ducks, loons, and Razorbills.

Return to the Polpis Road and continue on until you see Sesachacha Pond. There is a small pullover with room for two cars that gives a good view of the pond (8). Flocks of Greater Scaup, Buffleheads, Canvasbacks, Red-breasted Mergansers, Redheads, Surf and White-winged Scoters, and Common Loons gather here. Look for Great Cormorants as well as Great Blue Herons along the shore.

Farther around the pond there is another parking area. You can walk to a spot where an interesting sheltered cove can be studied. Green-winged Teal have been seen here.

In the afternoon, the light will be right to check out the gulls and waterfowl on the north end of Sesachacha Pond from Quidnet. The Quidnet Road goes to the right off the Polpis Road, 1.4 miles from the last parking area at Sesachacha.

It's also worthwhile to take the Pocomo Road off the Wauwinet Road over to Pocomo head (22). The last quarter mile of this road is dirt with potholes, but your reward is a marvelous view of the Head of the Harbor that is often teaming with waterfowl. If the tide is low there will be sandbars exposed that are prime shorebird resting-places. In the morning, the view across Nantucket Harbor towards town is marvelous. Here is a spot you may find a Barrow's Goldeneye in with the Commons. In the afternoon, looking east towards Wauwinet may provide good looks at Surf and White-winged Scoters. Don't forget to look at the sandbars across on Coatue. You may see a Northern Harrier or a Peregrine Falcon hunting over there as well.

On the way back to the Polpis Road, look for the 'Polpis Harbor Access' sign opposite #19 Wauwinet Road. This short dirt road takes you to the shore of Polpis Harbor, best viewed in the morning. Red-breasted Mergansers, Buffleheads, and sometimes a winter Kingfisher, can be seen here. There is also a visible Barn Owl box on a tripod about 0.25 miles down the shore on the right. Behind that is an Osprey Pole. Watch for Ospreys to arrive at the end of March.

On the way back to town, an interesting place to check is at the University of Massachusetts Boston Field Station at 180 Polpis Road. It is open from 7 a.m. to 9 p.m. every day and has many trails that provide good territory for winter landbirds. There are also excellent lookouts over Folger's Marsh with good morning light. Continuing on to the shore gives you excellent views of the upper harbor where you may find Brant and see the many species of salt water ducks that winter there.

Just 0.2 miles west of the Field Station is the parking lot for the Life Saving Museum (9). Here you can have an excellent look over a salt marsh for Hooded Merganser, American Bittern and many other specialties that wander in and out of this habitat. It is a great spot to find a winter Belted Kingfisher.

The brushy areas and cedars in this area are good for winter resident landbirds including Gray Catbird, Carolina Wren, or even a Baltimore Oriole. Cedar Waxwings and American Robins like this spot too.

Before calling it a day, take a look at Nantucket Harbor from the Great Harbor Yacht Club near town (10). There's usually a flock of 50 to a 100 Common Goldeneyes and Buffleheads and small flocks of Red-breasted Mergansers. Look for Ruddy Turnstones feeding in the washed up eel grass at the edge of the water. There are extensive mud flats here at low tide. The adjacent salt marsh, known as the 'Cricks,' is a spot that may harbor snipe and Nelson's Sparrows. Depending on the tide, the salt marsh can be treacherous, so don't go in there in your good shoes.

You might also look on the rocks at the Jetties Beach (23) for Purple Sandpipers and study the masses of gulls, cormorants, and eiders nearby. A few years ago you could find Harlequin Ducks close to the rocks and maybe they'll come back. Often there are Harbor Seals on the rocks at the far end. Don't go out on the rocks as they are slippery and the water can be like ice.

If you're interested in winter owls, the State Forest off the Old South Road (11) is a good place to look for Long-eared and Northern Saw-whet Owls.

Black-bellied Plover

Spring Birding on Nantucket

By the first week of April, the Piping Plovers have arrived on the outer beaches and the Horned Larks are getting ready to nest. Ospreys are active on the various nesting poles around the island. Gannets, Common and Red-throated Loons can still be seen in good numbers offshore. The Horned Grebes are acquiring their spring plumage. Follow the same routes given for winter.

It is now time to look for American Oystercatchers along the Jetties and at Eel and Jackson Points (4) and (25). Another good place to look from is Pocomo Point (22). Glossy Ibis might be seen in the salt marshes after a southerly storm.

Miacomet Pond (15) is an excellent spot to view waterfowl. If the pond is not frozen it makes a good winter trip as well. You can get good looks at Pied-billed Grebes, American Wigeons, scaup, Ring-necked Ducks, and Ruddy Ducks as well as Redheads, and an occasional Canvasback. To do this, you need to go out the Surfside Road.

This trip is best done with morning light. Start where Pleasant Street leads south from Main Street. From there it's 0.4 miles to where you find the five-corner intersection. From that stop sign you bear slightly to your right and you are on Atlantic Avenue that becomes Surfside Road. Then you continue 1.1 miles past the Nantucket Schools on your left until you reach Miacomet Road that turns to your right. Almost a mile down that road will bring you to an area where you can see Miacomet Pond on your right. There are a series of pull-offs here that allow excellent close-up viewing of Nantucket's waterfowl. For some reason, the birds seem more trusting here.

The paved road only goes about half way down the pond. From there on it is a heavily pot-holed dirt road that may challenge some vehicles. You don't actually need four-wheel drive to get to the parking lot near the barrier beach, but if you don't have high clearance you may want to leave your car and walk the remaining mile round-trip to the end of the pond. At the beach there is a good pelagic lookout for gannets, loons, sea ducks, and if you are extremely lucky, a Right Whale!

The spring land bird migration can be spectacular. Most warblers pass through during the month of May with the greatest abundance from the 15th to the 31st. The best places to look for

Wilson's Storm-Petrels

these in spring are in the towns of Nantucket and Siasconset. In Nantucket, follow the back lanes such as Ray's Court, Rose Lane, Cat Alley, Stone Alley, Gull Island, West Chester Street – wherever fruit trees are blooming and elms and maples are beginning to leaf out. Check out *"Birding Nantucket's Lanes, Alleys and Courts"* further on in this book. Now is a good time to visit the little Bird Sanctuary on North Beach Street where you may find Blue-gray Gnatcatchers and Ruby-crowned Kinglets in addition to various warblers and vireos.

In Siasconset, Main Street is good, not only for warblers but also Indigo Buntings and American Goldfinches on the grassy edge, and Rose-breasted Grosbeaks, both Baltimore and Orchard Orioles and Scarlet Tanagers in the trees overhead. Use the instructions in *"Birding 'Sconset's Lanes"* later in this book. This is a good time to take the 'Sconset Footpath. It starts near the Square and goes along the bluff nearly all the way to Sankaty Light (7), about 1.25 miles. There are fruit trees and tangles of honeysuckle, bayberry and wild rose where you might see Blackburnian, Black-throated Green, Northern Parula, Cape May, Bay-breasted, Blackpoll and even Cerulean Warblers. This is an excellent place to look since you are on the same level or above them, and can avoid that crick in the neck from looking up in tall trees. There is now only one spot where can enter or exit the Footpath, so remember that when you walk out on the path, you have to retrace your steps to get back out again. The path becomes impassable as you approach Sankaty due to erosion so you can no longer walk the whole distance.

If you want to do some night birding, take the Almanac Pond Road (13) off Polpis Road for a distance of one-half mile where you may hear American Woodcock, Whip-poor-will, and possibly Chuck-will's Widow and Saw-Whet Owl. There is a marshy area at the junction of the above two roads where you might hear Virginia Rails calling.

Northern Harriers

Summer and Fall Birding on Nantucket

By June, the migrants have gone and the local birds are nesting. Black-crowned Night-Herons nest near Long Pond (2), Quaise (14), and also, Coatue, where they have Snowy and Great Egrets for neighbors. Most any evening you will see them standing like sentinels on the shore of Long Pond or along the ditches of the salt marshes. Snowy Egrets are now breeding and can be seen on all of the salt marshes throughout the summer.

This is a good time to look for harriers. In years gone by, American Kestrels might be found, but they have become a rare sight on Nantucket. Take the Hummock Pond Road to the Miacomet Golf Course (15). Then follow the dirt road to the left and keep bearing left past the Clubhouse on the left toward Miacomet Pond. Anywhere along this road you used to be able to flush Short-eared Owls, especially during the early morning or at dusk. It's still worthwhile looking for them. You can follow this road to the ocean where, with luck and a spotting scope, you stand a chance of seeing shearwaters and possibly Wilson's Storm-Petrels. Follow the rutted road west to Hummock Pond Road at Cisco (21) and then return to town that way. Be careful as this area has been subjected to severe beach erosion over the past years. You may find some branches of the road vanishing onto the beach.

When you reach the paved (Cisco) road and you get to a clear vantage point, look west across Hummock Pond to see a high pole that has been erected on the other side. There is a platform that has been mounted at the top for use by nesting Ospreys. You will often see them in the air nearby or actually perched on the nest. Map reference point (24) refers to this spot. To get a really good look, walk the barrier beach until you are opposite the pole. An alternate method is to take the Massasoit Bridge Road from the Madaket Road that will approach this point from the north over an area known as the Head of the Plains.

Least Terns

Another summer trip would be to take the Madaket Road to the Eel Point Road (16). This becomes a rather rough dirt road as you approach Eel Point. It is good habitat for Red-tailed Hawks and Northern Harriers. It also used to be good Short-eared Owl and American Kestrel country. When you get to the parking area (4), leave your car and walk to the harbor shore. Also check out the "bathtub" (see instructions under *winter*) for cormorants, shorebirds, and gulls. You will find Savannah Sparrows in the upland and Saltmarsh Sparrows in the salt marsh. Oystercatchers can also be found in good numbers and Willets nest in the saltmarsh. Follow the road left past Warren's Landing (3) to return to the Madaket Road.

This area is an important staging area for terns in the spring and the fall as well as a nesting area for Least Terns. You may see huge numbers of terns resting on the sandbars of Eel Point. The small terns will be Leasts. Medium-sized terns include Common and Roseate. You may find Black Terns mixed in from mid-August through September. Be careful to obey the signs that restrict human activity that might disturb these birds.

There are also Least Tern nesting colonies on several beaches on the island's east end. The Coskata-Coatue Wildlife Refuge colony at Great Point continues to be posted. In recent years colonies have come and gone on Smith's Point and Tom Never's Head. Our shorelines are continually changing due to erosion and accretion. What is a successful colony one year may be washed away the next.

A good side trip is to go out the Polpis Road to Quaise Pasture Road marked (14) on the map. This starts out paved and

21

then turns to gravel. There is a loop at the end. At the two o'clock point on the loop, you will find the Masquetuck property of the Nantucket Conservation Foundation. This area has trails that lead to some excellent overlooks of Polpis Harbor and the salt marsh surrounding it. The woods there support uncommon nesting species like Great Crested Flycatcher, Black-and-white Warbler and American Restart. The marsh is a good spot for various types of herons that make Nantucket their home during the summer. It is also an interesting place to view salt-water ducks in the winter.

By mid-July the southward migration of shorebirds is underway. On Nantucket the shorebird migration is not as spectacular as the on Cape Cod because there are no extensive mudflats. Places to look are the following: Smith's Point (18); Eel Point (4); Great Point (17); Polpis harbor, approached from Pocomo or by boat at low tide when the birds are feeding; and the Creeks at the end of Washington Street Extension beyond the Great Harbor Yacht Club (10). The latter area is easily accessible from town and usually produces Black-bellied and Semipalmated Plover, Ruddy Turnstone, both Greater and Lesser Yellowlegs, Whimbrel, Pectoral, Semipalmated and Least Sandpipers, and Short-billed Dowitcher. For best light, either approach from Monomoy in the morning, or from the town side in the afternoon. There is a dike, the remains of the old railroad bed that runs from the Washington Street Extension to Orange Street, coming out next to the Spouter Pottery (now a school). On one side of the dike you have a view of the salt marsh where you may see Green Heron and various "peeps." On the other side, you can see the pond at Consue Springs with its aggregation of "puddle" ducks. Rails are possible along the edge.

The southwest shore of Sesachacha Pond (8) is good, particularly when the pond level is low. The Polpis Road runs close to a cove that is attractive to herons and ducks. The eastern section can be reached by walking along the beach from Hoick's Hollow (20) to the barrier beach that separates Sesachacha Pond from the ocean, or you can approach from the Quidnet side. A sandbar in the pond makes a good resting-place for cormorants, shorebirds, and gulls. As the pond is sometimes opened to the sea, the sandbar comes and goes.

The migration of land birds is often spectacular from August to October. The island is becoming wooded to such an extent that almost any grove of trees will draw songbirds. One of

22

the best areas is a small grove of pines called the Mothballs near the barrier beach at Cisco (21). This area has had all the pines destroyed due to a severe storm that contaminated them with salt. New growth is just starting to replace them. This is all privately owned but a road (Mothball Way) runs through the grove and by walking along here you can usually see most of the species. With a strong northwest wind it offers a lee. Warblers, vireos, wrens, flycatchers, kinglets, creepers, and sparrows stop here on their way south. There is a dirt road that diagonals to the left side of Cisco Road that takes you to an excellent parking lot. It is worthwhile to scan the ocean from here as you may see shearwaters.

A final area to be surveyed in autumn is Bartlett's Farm, Miacomet Golf Course (15), and surrounding farmland. Here you may see American Golden-Plover and Black-bellied Plover, Buff-breasted Sandpiper, Semipalmated Plover, and Killdeer as well as Merlin and Peregrine Falcon. Look for rare sparrows, such as Grasshopper and Lark in addition to the common ones. This is a good spot to look for other rarities such as Blue Grosbeaks, Yellow-headed Blackbirds, and Dickcissels.

Map of Selected Birding Localities

1 Maxcy's Pond
2 Long Pond
3 Warren's Landing
4 Eel Point
5 Madaket
6 Codfish Park
7 Sankaty Head Lighthouse
8 Sesachacha Pond
9 Life Saving Museum
10 The Boatyard
11 State Forest
12 Head of the Harbor

13 Almanac Pond Road
14 Quaise
15 Miacomet Golf Course
16 Eel Point Road
17 Great Point
18 Smith's Point
19 Siasconset Sewerbeds
20 Southeast Sesachacha
21 Cisco
22 Pocomo
23 Jetties Beach
24 Osprey Lookout
25 Jackson Point
P Pelagic Lookout
　Open Ocean Birds

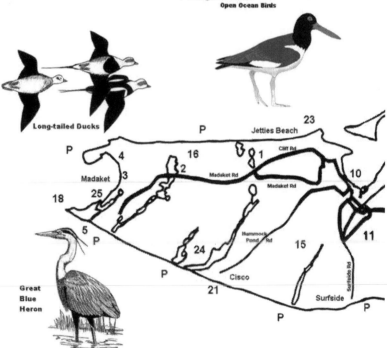

Long-tailed Ducks

Great
Blue
Heron

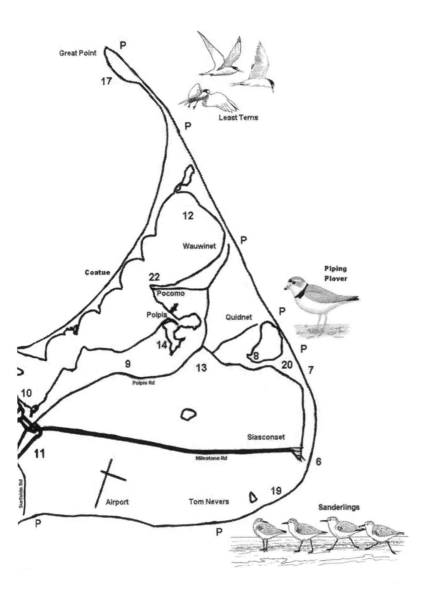

Great Point

P

17

Least Terns

12

Wauwinet

P

Coatue

22

Pocomo

Polpis

Piping
Plover

14

Quidnet

P

9

13

8

20

7

P

Polpis Rd

10

Siasconset

11

Milestone Rd

6

Surfside Rd

Airport

Tom Nevers

19

Sanderlings

P

P

Some Enjoyable Bird Walks Around Nantucket

Birding Nantucket's Lanes, Alleys, and Courts

This walk is described in three sections. You can walk them all at once, sequentially, or do them individually. Depending on how many birds you see, the whole journey will take two to three hours. Most of the birds described are likely in Nantucket's warmer months. What you find in the dead of winter is more problematic.

This first section of the walk starts at the foot of Main Street at the Pacific Club, with its historic quarterboards mentioning the ships from the Boston Tea Party -- *Dartmouth*, *Beaver*, and *Bedford* behind us. If you are a serious birder and up early, your

Northern Cardinal

view of Main Street may be fairly empty and bucolic. But during most of the day things are a little frantic here. Let's get away from that.

Walk up the left-hand side of Main, past Ralph Lauren. We'll show you how quickly you can escape the hustle and bustle of 'downtown' and get to the solitude of Nantucket's lanes.

Turn left on Union Street and walk to the south, crossing Salem Street and passing Force 5 Watersports. Already as you look

ahead past the Union Street Inn, you can feel a quieter mood. It's not too early to start listening to the bird calls coming from the ivy-covered bank above you – robins, cardinals and House Finches may be serenading you.

After you make a bend to the right, observe the picket fence on the right side of the street. There is a gap that leads into an ivy-trimmed cobblestone trail that is the beginning of Stone Alley. Stone Alley is easy to miss since the sign is often missing. Nonetheless it climbs the hill through the ivy, allowing you to do what any good birder desires – get your head up in the tree tops so

26

you can observe the birds at eye level without getting 'warbler neck.' Stop when you get to the stairs and look and listen for migrating warblers, vireos, and the like. You may hear the chatter of a Baltimore Oriole or the 'chip burr' of a Scarlet Tanager. This is a hot place for migrants. A lovely male Prothonotary Warbler visited near here a few years ago.

After you climb the stairs you are actually on the part of Stone Alley that is driveable with access up ahead to Orange Street. You can look up to the impressive clock tower of the Unitarian Church. Often you hear the mournful 'coo' of the Mourning Dove as you walk along here.

When you reach Orange, bear to your right across the street and proceed down the narrow alley on the right side of Hendrix Hall. This little alley will take you over to Fair Street. On the way you'll pass under a lovely pear tree that often harbors migrating warblers, vireos and orioles. You are crossing a little bird 'highway' of ornamental fruit trees that extends through these back yards starting with the stone Episcopal Church to the south and continuing right over this little walkway. Stop and listen and watch for birds moving in the leaves above you. You may notice horizontal rows of sapsucker wells drilled in the bark of some of these trees. Then walk on down the stairs past the lilac bush and out onto Fair Street.

Directly ahead of you, across the street, is Ray's Court. We'll walk down here, past the Fair Street Research Library of the Nantucket Historical Association. Ray's Court is very scenic, looking like a bit of England placed here, just a block off Main Street. We'll go past the Sylvia's Antiques and

Song Sparrow

the Carriage House Inn. Here is another good spot to stop and listen. The garden on the right looks inviting but it is private. Watch here for migrating thrushes and sparrows as well as the aforementioned songbirds. Follow the road is it curves sharply to the right and heads past a lovely apple tree to Main Street.

Walk across Main and then down Walnut Lane toward Liberty Street. When you get to Liberty, turn right and walk down to Centre and turn left, walking around the impressive architecture of the Methodist Church. This birdwalk is unintentionally becoming a church tour! On the right side of the church you will find Rose Lane, our next target.

Go up the lane, getting away from Centre Street's commotion, and soon you'll be on a lovely, grassy right-of-way between charming backyard gardens. Again, we have escaped the traffic noises and replaced them with bird calls. You can walk back on this lane until you reach the big board fence across it. Just be sure not to wander out onto people's lawns. You'll certainly find House Finches, cardinals, robins, and Song Sparrows. If you hit a migration day this is a great spot for warblers, vireos, orioles and tanagers. Be sure to listen for call notes.

Reverse your way back to Centre Street. This is the end of the first segment of the walk. You can see Main Street from here and the Pacific Club, your original starting point that is a few hundred yards to the east.

To start the second part of the walk, we head a few hundred yards to the left along Centre Street past the Jared Coffin House. Continue past Gay Street and Academy Lane until you reach the steps in front of the Old North (Congregational) Church. Walk up these steps and enjoy the imposing view of this lovely white spire reaching upwards above you. Glance up past the steeple to look for Chimney Swifts in the air. From April 15 until mid-October they course the air currents over Nantucket, feeding on insects before heading to South America for the winter.

There's a nice little area with benches adjacent to the head of the brick walkway that gives you a moment to rest and listen for the chip of a warbler. You can look for activity at eye-level in the trees along Centre Street.

Carolina Wren

Now, facing the front of the church, turn left and walk about one hundred feet down the lane to where Academy Lane intersects it. At that point you will see a sign that tells you that you've been on Church Court. Turn right and walk up Academy Lane. You'll undoubtedly hear the 'Hip hip hooray boys' of a Song Sparrow as you walk along here, and possibly the 'What cheer' of a bright red Northern Cardinal.

When you get to the end of Academy Lane, turn to your left and you'll be looking at a large red brick building where Ken attended his first eight grades of school back in the 40's and 50's. No longer used as a school, it is now an apartment building for Nantucket's senior citizens. Walk down past the gardens toward the school. Bear to your right and walk along the west side of the building. Here you have the opportunity to look over the bank down towards Lily Street and the Lily Pond below. This is a good spot to see warblers, vireos, and tanagers without developing 'warbler neck.' Not only do you not have to crane your neck, but you have a better chance of seeing them the way they are pictured in the field guide instead of viewing their bellies from beneath. This area abounds with House Finches and in season, Catbirds. It is a good spot to find a Ruby-crowned Kinglet when they are passing through in September or October.

Walk around the south end of the building and then down the steps into the parking lot. This is another good break point before starting into the Lily Pond area. You can walk back down Quince Street to Centre Street where you started.

Otherwise, turn to your right and you'll find a walkway to another set of steps that leads to a little road out to Lily Street. You may start hearing Red-winged Blackbirds as you approach the marshy area across the street. We'll now be venturing into the Lily Pond, a wonderful property that is part of the Nantucket Land Bank.

You can continue straight ahead down the lawn that is a right-of-way into the property. Keep on walking to the west and you'll come to a boardwalk that takes you through the low willow thicket in this very marshy stretch. This is a wonderful area for wrens. Surely you'll hear the Carolina Wren's 'tea-kettle, tea-kettle' here. People not named 'Shirley' may hear it as well.

When you get to the end of the boardwalk you'll be facing a cattail marsh where Wilson's Snipe have been flushed. This area is usually awash with red-wings and grackles. Deer often come here and you may notice their tracks in the mud. Turn to your right and cross the tiny footbridge, keeping the brushy area to your right. This area can be a magic spot for warblers, wrens, kinglets, catbirds, and even a kingbird.

29

Walk along the lawn at the edge of the brushy area as it gradually narrows to a path between tangles of rosebushes. Pause to look over the foliage and give a chance for a Common Yellowthroat to pop up. Listen for their 'chug' and make a 'spishhhhing' sound to entice them into view. Check out the tall trees to your left that may harbor an oriole, tanager, or grosbeak. Red-bellied Woodpecker, a good find on Nantucket, may nest near here.

The path ends at the foot of a drive that goes up the hill to your right. Check out the trees on both sides of this drive during migration for warblers and vireos. When you get to Lily Street, turn left and walk down to where it ends back on Centre. Here you turn to your left and walk past American Seasons Restaurant to Gull Island Lane, a small cobbled affair that travels about 50 yards in to your left. It is private beyond the fence, but if you walk along here it gives you an excellent view of a little triangular brushy area between here and West Chester Street that often is jumping with birds.

Black-capped Chickadees

Now go back and turn down West Chester. Look again into the brushy tangle between here and Gull Island Lane. With a different light pattern, you may pick up something you missed earlier.

Another hundred yards or so down West Chester brings us to Sunset Hill Road that goes off to the right with a sign directing you to the 'Oldest House' just up the hill. Turn right and walk up the grade and then continue onto the cobbled drive that actually goes into the Oldest House property. This junction point seems to be a hot spot for bird activity. Stop here and see what you can call in before walking along past the Oldest House itself. There are usually chickadees around and if you get them excited, other birds will often come in to see what is going on. The area around the Oldest House is a good spot to stop and take a break and give the birds a chance to pop up. Both Summer and Scarlet Tanagers have been seen here. Often you'll see a Mourning Dove perched atop the house. The house itself is quite interesting, having been built in 1686 by Tristram

Coffin. Ken's great great grandfather, Abner Turner, lived here in the 1850's.

There is a new park behind the Oldest House called Coffin Park. This can be an optional loop you can add. It is a wonderful wild and bushy area with trails and boardwalks that goes all the way to Cliff Road. It is great habitat for sparrows, wrens, and cardinals. Just be careful not to trespass onto the private property that bounds this park. When you finish this loop, return to the Oldest House.

Walk back to Sunset Hill Road through the gap in the split rail fence and then turn left to go back down the hill. As you do so, look into the backyard trees below you, taking advantage of your height to get an eye-level view of the birds therein. Resident species like cardinal, Song Sparrow, House Finch, flicker, Downy Woodpecker and even a mockingbird can be well observed this way.

Where the road joins West Chester, make a short right and then left on Wesco Place. This road is initially paved but reverts to a dirt road that ends back within the Lily Pond area. The point where the pavement ends is another birding activity hot spot as several habitats join here. There is a fresh water marsh to your right that may produce a Swamp Sparrow or Marsh Wren. Listen for the high-pitched "seeeeee" of the Cedar Waxwing. In migration, warblers, flycatchers, thrushes, and orioles like this area. Listen for the "potato chips" call of a goldfinch flying overhead.

There is a marked pathway that leads around some private property to bring you back into the main grassy area of the Lily Pond. From here you can see that you have made a loop. Go back out the way you originally came in, following the boardwalk up to Lily Street.

This ends our walk through Nantucket's alleys, lanes, and courts. You can either walk up past Academy Hill and then down Quince Street to Centre, or perhaps follow Lily to the right and then walk back along India Street to get back near your starting point.

Birding Nantucket's Wharves

Wharves are great for birdwatchers. With a long pier, you can walk to the middle of a body of water and see many birds that are not visible from shore. There are five major wharves protruding into Nantucket Harbor – from south to north, they are the Town Pier, Commercial Wharf, Old South Wharf, Straight Wharf, and Steamboat Wharf. These structures give you a great opportunity to see the birds of the harbor without a boat. I'm assuming you'll have a pair of binoculars and some sort of bird guide. A spotting scope will greatly help in picking out loons and cormorants in the distance.

You may be wondering if there's a difference between a wharf and a pier. A pier is a platform supported by pilings out over the water. A wharf is a place where boats may tie up and unload. So, a pier can actually be a wharf. Then there's a 'dock.' That's actually the area of water between two piers. You can walk along a dock, but it would require a miracle to actually walk 'on' the dock.

Ken walked all these wharves in blustery northerly winds towards the end of April and it took about an hour and a half. You can plan on that amount of time if you follow the same route. We'll cover the wharves from south to north because that uses the sunlight more effectively. The other factor you will want to consider is the tide. Some birds are best observed at high tide – others at low. We'll point out which ones and why.

We'll start at the foot of Main Street at the Pacific Club, facing the Horse Fountain. Turn left and head south, down Washington Street. Our first destination will be the Town Pier that is about a quarter mile distant. You'll pass Brant Point Marine just before you reach it. The actual Town Pier building has a sign on it saying "Shellfish and Marine Department." We're going to walk out to the end of the pier birding as we go.

If you don't already know whether the tide is up or down, look at the pilings along the wharf and check the water level compared to the high water mark. This will help you judge high or low. Or, if the harbormaster office is open, you can check the tide times right there.

This pier is interesting because you can actually get some beach views on both sides. Look at the piles of weed on the beach, another indication of the tide level. Often you will find turnstones or other sandpipers picking through them. There are usually Black Ducks and Mallards along the shore as well. Learn to distinguish the Black Ducks by their yellow bills compared to the female Mallards' orange bill with the brown saddle. The green-headed drakes are easy. These ducks also like to sit on the rafts that are moored nearby.

Don't be surprised if the walking surface is covered with broken shells. The Herring Gulls, those are the ones with the light gray wings, have learned to fly high up and then drop shells so they'll break and give up the tasty morsels within. Herring Gulls are the most common of our gulls. Get familiar with their size and shape. They vary greatly in plumage from the almost solid brown of the first year birds to the silver and white of the four-year-olds. Their scientific name, *Larus argentatus*, actually means 'silver gull.'

This wharf is also a likely place to hear and see Least Terns. These small, gray, black, and white 'sea swallows' often feed in the south end of the harbor. Listen for their strident high calls as they fly by, occasionally plunging into the water for a minnow, then rising, shaking their feathers as they do so. Least Terns are a threatened species and Nantucket is one of the best places to see them.

If you do this walk after the end of May, the winter ducks will probably be gone. In the chilly months,

Buffleheads

33

the harbor teems with Buffleheads, Goldeneye, Red-breasted Mergansers, and often Eider and Long-tailed Duck. You still may find some non-breeding stragglers hanging around the docks.

A summer bird to watch for is the Belted Kingfisher. Its call is described as like bones rattling inside a glass jar. I've never personally rattled bones in a glass jar, but this description really gets the idea across. The call normally lasts a few seconds and if you follow the sound, you'll see a pigeon-sized bird with a rather large, shaggy head. Perhaps it will land atop one of the lamp poles along the pier. From here he'll stare down at the water, looking for a fish on which to dive. Sometimes they hover over a particular spot of water before plunging in for a meal. Kingfishers do not swim, so they've got to get quickly out of the drink or they'll become fish food themselves.

As you walk along the pier you will hear the '*coos*' of Rock Pigeons beneath your feet. These are the same as the city 'park pigeons.' For some reason, they love the wharf environment and you'll see great flocks of them, powering their way through the air. Sometimes a similar-sized bird, the Peregrine Falcon, will make a pass through the flock and pick off a meal. However you are not likely to see that happen during the summer months.

It's about a hundred yard walk to the end of the pier where it 'tees.' When you get to the end, look in the water for Double-crested Cormorants. These rather sinuous-looking birds swim around in the harbor and dive for fish.

If you are here in the winter, check the outer edge of the wooden platform where Ruddy Turnstones and Purple Sandpipers like to rest.

Now let's hike back in from the pier and turn to the right, down Washington Street and head for Commercial Wharf. Turn right on Commercial Street and go east, past the site on the left where Nantucket used to generate its electricity. Now there are just the fuel tanks to remind us of that day.

Check out the little abutment off to the right where you can have another view of the beach and also look at

Ruddy Turnstones

the water along the south edge of the wharf. This is another good place to see Black Ducks, Mallards, and perhaps a Pied-billed Grebe, diving headfirst or submerging slowly, submarine style.

Walk along the sidewalk between the gray-shingled shanties until you reach wooden part of the wharf. Then turn right and follow the pier. Here I'll point out another common gull of the harbor – the Great Black-backed. This gull is larger than the Herring, jet-black replacing the silver gray on the back. It is also a 'four year' gull, taking that amount of time to reach adult plumage. The young Great Black-backeds are more mottled and never as brown as the young Herrings.

Bear left and walk to the end of the dock. Along the outside edge, check the ledges down near the water. If it is high tide, you may find Purple Sandpipers and Ruddy Turnstones taking shelter there. Their normal habitat is the jetties at the entrance to the harbor, but if it's at all windy at high tide, they take refuge here. The Purples are generally gone by the end of May, but you may get lucky.

Now walk back towards the shore, this time walking along the right side of the buildings with the basin between this wharf and Old South Wharf on your right. Check the water there for straggling winter ducks.

Walk to the right along the cobbles of New Whale Street. The fuel tanks will be to your left and the sign for the Nantucket Ship Chandlery directly in front. Bear to the right on the brick walk underneath the Nantucket Angler's Club, then turn to your right and walk out the edge of the wharf. When you get to the sign that says "Private Yachtsmen and their Guests Only" swing around and head back down the north side of the wharf. There are some flowering cherry trees along the edge of the Grand Union Market parking lot that are worth checking out as you walk over to Straight Wharf.

This may be a busy place if you're not here very early in the morning. There are many shops and the 'fast' boat, *Gray Lady*, docks here. Walk up the right hand side past all the sport fishing boats waiting there to take you out to catch that big

Laughing Gull

Bluefish or Striper! When you get to the end of the wooden deck, bear to your left onto the red brick path and approach the wooden pier that goes out around the end of the marina.

Walk out to the east as far as you can. The main treat here is to check out the rock bed to the north where the old wharf used to be. At high tide the rocks are hidden, but at other times, they are the resting-place for many interesting birds. You may find two species of gull here that have black heads – the dark mantled, Laughing Gull or the small silver backed Bonaparte's. Ring-billed Gulls can also be seen here. Other birds sometimes seen on these rocks include oystercatchers, terns, egrets, night-herons and even cormorants, drying their wings. Turnstones often pick their way around the barnacles.

At the end of the wharf, scan the waters in the middle of the harbor for cormorants and perhaps a late Common Loon. Then head back in. If nature is calling, there are bathrooms on the right-hand side of the building at the end of the wharf. If the *Gray Lady* is in, you'll be walking past it at this point. Walk through the shops back down the wharf, being sure to check out the trees as you go by. During migration you may often see some quite exotic warblers in these trees.

Bear to the right past the bandstands and the Nantucket Provisions sandwich shop and head through the archway and continue down the cobblestone street. Here you may see the resident cardinals, robins, and perhaps hear a Song Sparrow. You'll reach a major paved cross street that is Easy Street. Walk to your right, down Easy, past the entrance to Old North Wharf that is private.

Shortly you'll come to a section where you walk right past the water. If the tide is low, a fair-sized beach appears with some interesting mud flats. You can see yellowlegs here and several species of 'peep' if your timing is right. More normally there will be some Black Ducks and Mallards feeding here – occasionally a Mute Swan will be swimming in this little basin, known as 'Still Dock.'

Our last wharf is Steamboat Wharf where the big car ferries come in from the mainland. We'll turn right past the restaurant at the corner and walk out. Even quite early in the morning this place is a beehive, since folks have to drive here around 6 a.m. in order to queue for the first crossing. Your best chance for good birding here might be just after the 6:30 a.m. boat leaves.

Walk along the right-hand side, checking out the docks for a lingering Red-breasted Merganser. Continue along the right side, again checking the rocks at the end of Old North Wharf. You may be able to see a bird from this side that was obscured before. Be sure to look at birds sitting on top of the pilings, don't just assume they are all Herring Gulls.

When you get to the end, walk to the left along the edge. If the boat is not there, you have a good view to the left, across the inlet, to Children's Beach and the White Elephant Hotel. This is another area where ducks feed. I've seen lines of mergansers chase a school of fish in there to trap them in the shallows. They make an exciting scene, dashing this way and that across the water before plunging under for a meal.

Then head back towards shore with the impressive spire of the old North Church on the horizon before you. Directly ahead is the Whaling Museum with its wonderful displays about these huge mammals and the methods used by early Nantucketers to catch them and extract their oil. You can go in, watch an interesting lecture, and then write some notes about the wonderful birds that I hope you've just seen during our walk around Nantucket's wharves.

Birding 'Sconset's Lanes

Siasconset is a lovely village on the east end of Nantucket Island. Seven and one half miles from downtown Nantucket Town, it was originally a collection of fishing shacks in the 1700s, then discovered by the New York theater people in the late 1800s. It has grown to be the charming collection of rose-covered cottages that it is today. The full name, Siasconset, recognizes one of the early Nantucket Indian chiefs, but now most people simply refer to it as 'Sconset.

The center of 'Sconset is the flagpole and circle in front of the Post Office. We'll start our walk in Codfish Park (6), the area below the bank where the tide sweeps the Atlantic Ocean back and forth. You get there by following Gully Road under the footbridge. There is a little parking lot to the right where you can leave your car or bicycle.

In the area adjacent to that little parking lot there is a grove of scrub pines near the beach that graduates into hardwood scrub and a few flowering fruit trees as you approach the bluff. This area often harbors many landbird migrants. During migration you may

House Finch

find almost any species of warbler or vireo here as well as grosbeaks, orioles, catbirds, and tanagers. At any time of the year there are likely to be chickadees, Red-breasted Nuthatches, Song Sparrows, and House Finches here. From September through early May you may see a Merlin, or Sharp-shinned Hawk hunting through here.

Approach the footbridge and then climb the stairs to the left. As you climb these stairs you are actually climbing into the foliage of the trees nearby and have the opportunity to see birds intimately at eye-level. Birders strive to find these opportunities to see otherwise skulking species well.

Once you walk off the bridge – head down Ocean Avenue, walking south along the bluff. Here you can also have a fine aspect of the ocean to the east. Perhaps you'll see the white shape of a

Northern Gannet fishing over one of the rips. You'll undoubtedly hear the songs of resident robins, Song Sparrows, cardinals and perhaps a House Finch.

Walk along and turn right on Cottage Avenue, past the charming rose-covered cottages. There are wonderful privet hedges along here that often harbor migrants in season. This is the territory of a particularly versatile mockingbird. This bird is very clever in making you think you are hearing a Carolina Wren, cardinal, towhee, or even a yellowthroat. Be sure to peek at the lawns to look for Indigo Buntings hopping in the grass. Look for Song Sparrows, nesting robins, cardinals, and House Finches.

When you get to the end of Cottage, turn left on Laurel and walk behind the Summer House. At the end of that street, turn right, going against the 'One-way' street sign and head west, down picturesque, shell-covered, Magnolia. Again, you are in a wonderful area for birds, lots of cover with big privet hedges on both sides of the road. Stop every now and then and look for movement in the bushes, your first clue that a foraging warbler may be present.

Northern
Mockingbird

If you are early in the morning, before everyone else wakes up, you can find wonderful birds hopping around the lawns here. We've seen Chipping, Field, and White-crowned Sparrows, Indigo Buntings, and many other small finches here. You'll pass a house on the left named for a bird we'd all like to see – 'The Good Tern.'

At the next intersection, we'll turn right on McKinley Avenue and head to the north. Again, we'll have privet hedges on both sides of us and interesting lawns to look into. You'll probably hear the call of the House Finch here and perhaps a Goldfinch in song, maybe a Cardinal, certainly the song of a robin. Just past Grand Avenue there is a particularly interesting yard on the right. There are fine open lawn spaces surrounded by shrubbed areas on the sides, where we've seen Indigo buntings in the past. It's also a good place to look for migrant sparrows – White-crowns, White-throats, maybe a Chipping or Field Sparrow.

When you reach the end of McKinley Avenue, turn left onto Milestone Road, also known as Main Street in 'Sconset. Here there is a nice, grassy berm with tiny daisies on both sides of the pavement that is a good habitat for small finches to forage. Across the street you'll see a lovely house with cream-colored trim, a widow's walk on the roof, and a beautiful stone chimney at number 27. In the front yard, on the left side, is one of the most famous bird-watching spots on Nantucket – the flowering cherry tree. This tree flowers early in the spring and serves as a magnet for early orioles, tanagers, and Rose-breasted Grosbeaks. The list of birds that have been seen in this tree is truly awesome. Please don't trespass in the yard and respect the privacy of the owners who have been somewhat nonplused in the past to find large numbers of people training binoculars, seemingly in their front windows.

As we continue west on the Milestone Road, the trees on both sides have been good for various woodpeckers, and hole-nesting birds such as nuthatches and chickadees.

Our first right is West Sankaty Avenue (marked School Street at the other end) and we'll walk along there, heading north. The first house on the corner is called 'Laughing Gull.' It would be fun sometime to walk 'Sconset's streets and just see how many birds you could check off by looking at the names on the houses. You'll see a house on the right called 'Time Out', and behind that house on the left, is another early-flowering cherry tree that should be checked out in the early spring for orioles, tanagers, and grosbeaks. We'll walk past an interesting building on the left that at one time was 'Sconset's one-room schoolhouse. Ken's grandmother attended school here in the early 1900s. Now it houses the fire trucks.

Rose-breasted Grosbeak

Turn right on New Street and walk down to the east. On the north corner here, you will see a very interesting stand of bamboo. This lot has a lot of cover on it and, while you are unlikely to see a panda, you will certainly see a great number of birds. Unfortunately during most seasons, they will be predominately grackles, but there's often a mockingbird around here and if it is migration time, most any landbird can be found here.

The 'Sconset chapel on the right, has a wonderful churchyard garden next to it. You can walk in through the gate on the right hand side and proceed along the slate walkway. Look particularly at the tall privet hedge at the back where some interesting migrants can often surprise you. Many times we have found Indigo Buntings back here as well as Rose-breasted Grosbeaks and all manor of migrating sparrows.

If there are no services going on, you can walk around the front of the church and through the hedge out onto Chapel Street that runs between New Street and Milestone Road. There is an interesting little umbrella pine tree adjacent to the side entrance where a Northern Saw Whet Owl sat one winter. The area right near this entrance is also a good birding spot, providing you get there before the tennis matches start up across the street. In the spring, sapsuckers and creepers have been found in these trees. Notice the horizontal rows of sapsucker work in the bark.

Now we walk back to New Street and head between the 'Sconset Casino, a private club, on the right, and the Chanticleer, a trendy restaurant, on the left.

At the end of New Street, where Folger's Court joins it, you reach two important places. The first is the only public restroom facility in 'Sconset, and the second is historical -- the 'Sconset town pump. This unimposing little wooden structure sits in a square and is the site of the original pump from 1776.

Two nice cherry trees on the east (Center Street) side of this square should always be checked as they often harbor migrating warblers and vireos.

Go ahead and proceed to the left, walking down Center, past the interesting cottages, checking out the hedgerows on the way, all the time listening for bird calls.

We'll cut through on Mitchell Street and walk toward a cottage called 'Mizzentop' with a dark green trim. We'll then walk to the right of that cottage, heading toward the beach and turn left on a shell-covered, rutted lane that will take us to the 'Sconset Footpath. This may seem like a tight little lane but quite often we find small sparrows and finches working the grass on either side.

41

Next to house number 21 you'll see a paved walkway going to the right with a metal post next to it. This leads us to the beginning of the actual 'Sconset Footpath that goes off to the left. This path proceeds about 0.75 miles toward Sankaty Lighthouse. Walking on this path is described in the section under '*Spring Birding.*' However, for this walk we'll be staying on the paved walkway here and head down the bank, back into Codfish Park.

As we do this, we have another opportunity to look into the tops of the trees below us. Pause a moment and listen and look for any birds moving there. This is a great chance to see migrating songbirds. We are also walking into an area that has produced some really interesting birds in the past – Blue Grosbeak for instance. This area is just beyond where the path curves to the right and joins Bank Street. This spot, just ahead, has a nice little hardwood habitat around a big sycamore maple tree. Listen here for the call of the Carolina Wren, catbird, House Finch, Song Sparrow and goldfinch, to mention a few.

At this point, you have two choices. You can walk straight ahead and then along the beach until you reach the area where you parked – or you can walk along Bank Street, checking out the interesting cover that is growing on the side of the bluff to your right. Bank Street is an area through which migrants seem to like to move for some reason. This is often a good spot to see thrashers, catbirds, and even warblers and vireos, working the ground for grubs and insects along this bluff.

It's probably a few hundred yards to where the road bends to the left to join Codfish Park Road. This is right next to a house called 'The Cuckoo's Nest.' The people who named this may have been European, since there the cuckoo is a parasite, not actually building a nest, and the name would be full of irony. Or maybe they're just 'cuckoo.' The two new-world cuckoos you might see on Nantucket – Yellow-billed, or Black-billed – do build nests and it's just possible to see one passing through Codfish Park during migration.

Bonaparte's Gulls

Here on the beach, you see some big pipes going this way and that – the de-watering system that is supposed to be saving this area from further erosion. The Atlantic Ocean, here looming beyond the beach, provides a 3,000-mile reach to Spain. Check out this area for all kinds of seabirds from Long-tailed Ducks, three species of scoters, eider, various alcids, loons, grebes, and gannets. At times, this area teems with gulls, and it is one of the best places in New England to see Lesser Black-backed and Iceland Gulls. From October through February, the flocks of Bonaparte's Gulls often number in the thousands. Sometimes Little Gulls and Black-headed Gulls from Europe are with them.

American Redstarts

The ocean is always changing depending on the tide and the wind. Most of this walk is best done in the early morning to have the light behind you. However, afternoon and evening are the best times to look out over the ocean. Always try and use the light to your advantage when birding.

The area to the right, behind the little area with playground equipment, is good to check in the morning. We often find early migrating Common Yellowthroats, Yellow Warblers, and Indigo Buntings in this brush.

Now you should be back where you started. I hope you've had a nice walk and perhaps added a bird to your life, or at least your year list. At the very least you should have had a delightful walk through the charming village of 'Sconset.

Summary

In Birding Nantucket our aim has been to show you what we consider to be the best and most accessible bird spots, whether you have a car or are on foot. If you find some haunts on your own that you like as well, the authors are always interested in hearing of such places.

During the summer months, the Maria Mitchell Association conducts bird walks and will arrange a sea trip for anyone interested in pelagics. If you would rather arrange your own trip, check the yellow pages of the telephone book under Boats, Rental and Charter.

Herring Gulls

Accidentals

Those species for which there are five or fewer 'live' records over the past 50 years have been placed on the Accidental List. The initials of the first observers and those who confirmed the identification are given with names listed below; # indicates other observers; * denotes specimen. Specimens are in the collection of the Maria Mitchell Association unless otherwise noted.

FULVOUS WHISTLING DUCK. Flock of 6 shot 27 Nov. 1979, * GJD; 7 Nov. 1986, DB.

GREATER WHITE-FRONTED GOOSE. 11 – 30 June 2008, SM#; 10 Jan. 2009, DL#.

ROSS'S GOOSE, 11 Dec. 2010 – 17 Feb. 2011, JT#. 4 April 2014, PP.

TUFTED DUCK. 16, 18 Feb. 1975, HC #, 13 Jan. – 6 Apr. 1997, NB #; 2 March – 11 April, 2013, ER #.

PACIFIC LOON. 18 May 2008, EVL #; 12-31 Dec. 2011, EVL #; 6 Jan. 2013, EVL#.

WESTERN GREBE. 28 – 30 Dec. 1979, JS #; 2, 3 Jan. 1982, OK #, 30, 31 Dec. 1983 – 1 Jan. 1984, SP #.

YELLOW-NOSED ALBATROSS, 29 May 2005, RRV.

BAND-RUMPED STORM-PETREL. 28 Aug. 2011, RRV, EVL;

WHITE-TAILED TROPICBIRD. 13 Sept. 1960, 1 immature * in PMS, BSH; 14 Sept. 1960, 1 adult *, JMA.

RED-BILLED TROPICBIRD, 2 May 2003, 1 (Muskeget) IN.

AMERICAN WHITE PELICAN. 2 July 1950, EC #; 22 Oct. – 4 Dec. 1974, JVD #; 12 – 13 Sept. 2010 VC #.

BROWN PELICAN. 12 – 14 Jan. 1998, ET #; July 2000, ER; June 4, 2011, CW; 26 June 2012, from ferry near Jetties; ??; Oct. 31 – Nov. 4, 2012, EVL#.

MAGNIFICENT FRIGATEBIRD. 5 July – 8 Sept. 1951, KS #; 11, 12 May 1969, SF #; 9 Oct 2006, SP#; 20 – 22 Oct. 2011, JBC #.

LEAST BITTERN. 6 April 1958, RF, photo; 24 Aug. 1982, SP.

LITTLE EGRET. 14 May into Aug. 1992, SP #; 15 May into Aug. 1993, SP #; 16 May 1998, SP #; 28 May 2005, RRV; 21 May – 6 Aug. 2006, ER#.

WESTERN REEF HERON. 26 April – 13 Sept. 1983, RR #.

WHITE IBIS. 18 Feb. 1965 *, EFA; Aug. 1979 CC; 19 Aug. 1982, CB #.

SWAINSON'S HAWK. 5 Sept. 1979, NC.

GOLDEN EAGLE. 20, 21 April 1957, PBH #; 31 Aug. 1961 PBH #; 11 Nov. 1962, JCA #, found dead 15 Nov. 1962, * RM; 25 June 1985, PCB.

YELLOW RAIL. 31 Dec. 1984, OK; 17,19 Jan. 2000 FG; 28 Nov. 2000, ER; 19 Jan. 2002, KTB; 29–30 Dec. 2006, RRV#.

BLACK RAIL. 31 Mar. 1978, * BB; 31 Dec. 2005, RVV.

PURPLE GALLINULE. 14, 15 May 1984, SN #; 6 May 1993, * M&SR; 11 June – 4 July 1997 PCB #; 12 July – 2 Aug. 1998, AS #; 23 June 2009 PCB#.

NORTHERN LAPWING. 30 Oct. 2012 – 1 April 2013, EVL#.

WILSON'S PLOVER. 11 June 2005, ER; 2 Sept. 2009, PP; 28 March 2010, ER?.

AMERICAN AVOCET. 26 April 1977, EFA #; 17 Aug. 1985, JPE #; 7 Oct. 2002, ER; 12 - 24 Oct. 2007, SL#.

GRAY-TAILED TATTLER. 18 – 20 Oct. 2012, SP#.

BAR-TAILED GODWIT. 23 Sept. – 4 Oct. 1978, WRP #; 7 – 9 June 2012, RRV.

CURLEW SANDPIPER. 26 Sept. 1971, JMT; 4, 5 Aug. 1979, 1 adult, KH #; 15 July 1984, HRS & AE.

RUFF. 12-13 April 2014, JT #.

LONG-BILLED DOWITCHER. 15 March 1981, SP; 11 Dec. 2001, KTB#. Nov. 5 – 12, 2012, EVL & ER.

LONG-TAILED JAEGER. 22 Sept. 1951, JCA; 31 May 1972, from Steamer, EFA; 17 Sept. 1976, GLS #; 31 May 2008, EVL#.

GREAT SKUA. 10 Oct. 1958, JCA; 27 Sept. 1970, BBC; 10, 11 Jan. 1979, GF #; 21 Nov. 1991, one dead, JCA #.

SOUTH POLAR SKUA. 15 June 2009, RRV; 20 June 2011, RRV; 21 June 2011, EVL. 11 June 2011, RRV

FRANKLIN'S GULL. 9 – 12 June 1982, ABF #.

MEW GULL. 2 – 15 Oct. 1964, JCA #; 4 Jan. 1981, RRV #; 28, 29 Sept. 1981, SP; 30 Dec. 2013 – 2 Jan. 2014, PD #.

CALIFORNIA GULL. 3 Jan. – 4 June 2005, PD#; 5 Jan. – 3 Feb. 2006, ER #.

THAYER'S GULL. 26 Dec. 1980 – 27 Feb. 1981, RRV #; Jan. 1998, RRV; Jan. 1999, RRV; 17 Mar. 1999, KTB.

GULL-BILLED TERN. 30 April 1982, EFA #; 11 April 1983, SP #.

BRIDLED TERN. 8 Sept. 1952, RWS#; 7 Sept. 1979, TH; 17 July 2000, RRV#; 28 Aug. 2011, RRV.

BROWN NODDY. 27 Aug. 1957, PBH #, photo.

BAND-TAILED PIGEON. 22 – 26 June 1996, FP #.

EUROPEAN TURTLE-DOVE. 20 July 2001, RRV *

EURASIAN COLLARED-DOVE, 14 – 15 May 2011, SL #.

CHUCK-WILL'S-WIDOW. 19 June – mid Aug. 1973, SP #; 24 May – Mid Aug. 1974, SP #; late May – mid Aug. 1975, SP #; 21 June 1983, JVD.

BLACK-CHINNED HUMMINGBIRD. 15 Oct. - 12 Nov. 2007, EVL#. 20 Oct. 2013, EVL#.

CALLIOPE HUMMINGBIRD. 19 – 22 October 2013, RP#.

ALLEN'S HUMMINGBIRD. 26 Aug. 1988 * MCZ, WHB.

RUFOUS/ALLEN'S HUMMINGBIRD. Oct. 4, 2012 – Jan. 5, 2013 KKP.

BLACK-BACKED WOODPECKER. 21 Oct. 1922, JF; 24 Nov. 1964, EVD #. 31 Dec., 1972 – 1 Jan. 1973, RRV; 2 – 26 Apr. 2009 MP#.

GYRFALCON. 10 Feb. 1985, gray phase, DB and GP; 5 May 1987, * DB; 12 Dec. 2011 EVL #.

CAVE SWALLOW. Nov. 11 and Nov. 19, 2008, EVL. Nov. 2, 2012 DDF.

ACADIAN FLYCATCHER. 28 May 1980, EFA #, Banded; 12 Sept. 1983, EFA #, Banded; 25 May 1987, banded EFA #.

SAY'S PHOEBE. 8 Oct. 1977, HLJ; 24 Sept 1980, HS #.

ASH-THROATED FLYCATCHER. 12 Nov. 2011, SL #; 25 Nov. 2011, EVL #; 27 Nov. 2011, PP #.

FORK-TAILED FLYCATCHER. 16 – 18 Sept. 1982, MH #; 24 - 25 May 2002, RK#, 12–13 July 2003, KB#; 18–19 May 2005, VF #; 8 May 2009, DL.

LOGGERHEAD SHRIKE. Formerly rare spring and fall migrant. Last record Sept. 1972, RRV.

EURASIAN JACKDAW. 29 Nov. 1982 – 4 April 1983, SP #; 23 June 1983, DC; 31 Dec 1983 – 2 Jan 1984, GdE #; 9 July 1984, NJJ #.

FISH CROW. 30 Dec. 2006, RVV#; 30 April 2007, KTB; CBC CW bird for 2007; 30 May 2009, KTB.

COMMON RAVEN. 22 FEB. 2014, EVL #.

TOWNSEND'S SOLITAIRE, 22 – 23 Oct. 2011, EVL #.

VARIED THRUSH, 7 Oct. 1999, JH#; 30 Jan. 2004 – 18 Mar. 2004, EFA; 30 – 31 Dec. 2004, BC#.

PHAINOPEPLA. 11 – 16 Feb. 1973, JCA #.

CHESTNUT-COLLARED LONGSPUR. 25 – 27 Oct. 1979, 1 banded, RRV # photo.

BLACK-THROATED GRAY WARBLER, 1 – 4 Feb.2007, EFA #; 14 Oct. 2013, EVL#.

MACGILLIVRAY'S WARBLER. 4 Sept 1983, 1 banded, RS #.

HENSLOW'S SPARROW. 11 Oct. 1979, RRV #.

LECONTE'S SPARROW. 7 Oct. 1980 RRV #.

LARK BUNTING. 23 – 26 May 1982, 1 female, PG; 8 – 11 Sept. 1997, NB #.

SEASIDE SPARROW. 22 Dec. 1979 - 2 Jan. 1980, RRV#; 6 Sept. 1999, KH; 6 Oct. 2000, RN.

HARRIS' SPARROW. 27 – 28 Nov. 1967, BR #; 25 Oct. – 5 Nov. 1968, JCA #.

BLACK-HEADED GROSBEAK. 3 Jan. – 24 April 1956, KTB #; 27 Oct. 1979, RRV #.

LAZULI BUNTING. 5 - 10 May 2002, NS #.

PAINTED BUNTING. 17 – 25 April 1961, VR #; 17 – 20 Nov. 1963, BR *; 2 – 8 Dec. 2011, VA #.

BREWER'S BLACKBIRD. 7, 8 Oct. 1977, EVD, KH #; 3 April 1978, EFA #.

PINE GROSBEAK. 23, 27 Jan. & 12 Feb. 1960, EFA; 25 Nov. 2007, ER

HOARY REDPOLL. 20 March 1982, BBC; 8 Feb. 2008, EVL; 29 Dec. 2008 PD #.

Names of Observers

J. Clinton Andrews, Marcia Aguiar, Edith F. Andrews, James M. Andrews, Virginia Andrews, William H. Baltosser, Bruce Bartlett, John W. Bartlett, Christos Bazakas, Douglas Beattie, Paul Bennett, David Berry, Kenneth T. Blackshaw, Richard Bowen, Brookline Bird Club, Nick Brooks, Kathy Butterworth, Phyllis C. Burchell, V. Calarco, Jeff Carlson, Brian Chadwick; Nancy Clafflin, Edward Coffin, Harold Connor, Carroll Crocker, Davis Crompton, Alfred Crosby, Peter Cull, Jenn Decker, John V. Dennis, Greg J. Derr, Patrick Dugan, Peter W. Dunwiddie, Dana Duxbury-Fox, Glen d'Entrement, John P. Ebersole, Jesse Eldridge, Alexander Ellis, J. H. Farley, Anthony B. Farrell, Chester Faunce, Sheila Faunce, Virginia Finlay, Chris Floyd, Kirby Fowler, Richard Ford, H. Crowell Freeman, Granger Frost, Sam Fusaro, N. Gallagher, Frank Gallo, Patricia Gardner, Ida Giriunas, Ted Godfrey, Kenneth Harte, John Hayden, Susan Henning, Beatrice S. Heywood, Philip B. Heywood, Maria Holt, Timothy Holt, John Hoye; Nan Jenks-Jay, H. Lawrence Jodrey, Robert Kennedy, Ollie Komar, Diane Lang, Steve Langer, E. Vernon Laux, Jerry Light, Ron Light, Marcia Litchfield, Earle R. MacAusland, Robert Marks, C. Russell Mason, Beverly McLaughlin, Joshua Murphy, Sean Murphy, Museum of Comparative Zoology, Ian Nisbet, Sherley Newell, Rick Newman, Patricia Pastuszak, Peabody Museum of Science, Francis Pease, Blair Perkins, Geddes Perkins, Juliet Perkins, Michelle Perkins, Simon Perkins, Wayne R. Petersen, Katherine K. Pochman, Richard Prum, Edie Ray, Victor Reed, Betty Reyes, Robert Ridgley, Mark Ryan, Katherine Seeler, Henry Seibert, Henry R. Sheets, Jay Shetterly, Al Silva, Nonie Slavitz, Robert W. Smart, Gerald L. Soucy, Jim Stewart, Robert Stymeist, Joseph M. Taylor, Ellen Tonkin, Jeremiah Trimble, Peter Trimble, Elizabeth Van Duyne, Richard R. Veit, Barbara Vigneau, Clark Whitcomb.

The Maria Mitchell Association offices are at 4 Vestal Street, Nantucket, MA 02554. Phone: 508 228-9198. On the web at www.mmo.org

Greater
Shearwaters

51

Habitat Distribution Map

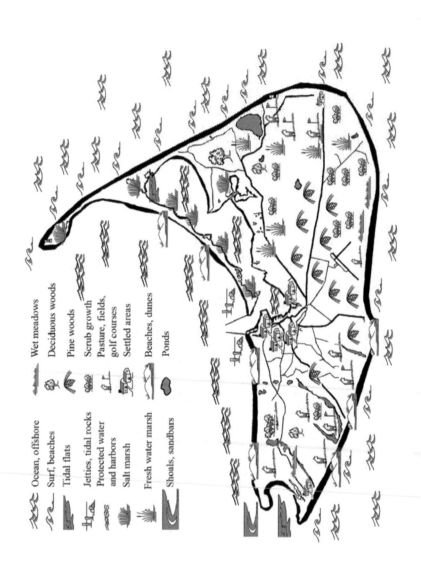

Ocean, offshore
Surf, beaches
Tidal flats
Jetties, tidal rocks
Protected water and harbors
Salt marsh
Fresh water marsh
Shoals, sandbars

Wet meadows
Deciduous woods
Pine woods
Scrub growth
Pasture, fields, golf courses
Settled areas
Beaches, dunes
Ponds

Key To Bar Charts

Birds are classified in the following categories:

ABUNDANT – difficult to avoid seeing

VERY COMMON – usually seen in good numbers

COMMON – easy to find

UNCOMMON – present but must be looked for

RARE – not seen every year

▬▬▬▬▬▬▬▬	Abundant
■■■■■■■■■■■■■■■	Very Common
══════════	Common
──────────	Uncommon
··················	Rare
< >	Breeding: Beginning End
≪ ≫	Erratic breeding

Habitat Codes

A – Ocean, offshore
B – Ocean Beaches and surf
C – Tidal Flats
D – Jetties and tidal rocks
E – Harbors
F – Ponds
G – Salt and brackish marshes
H – Fresh marshes and swamps
I – Wet Meadows

J – Deciduous woods
K – Pine Woods
L – Scrub Growth
M – Fields, pastures
N – Settled Areas
O – Beaches and Dunes
P – Nantucket Sound

S – Shoals and sandbar

COMMON NAMES	HABITAT	JAN	FEB	MAR	APR	MAY	JUN	JUL	AUG	SEP	OCT	NOV	DEC
Snow Goose	F M												
Canada Goose	E F G H M												
Brant	B E												
Mute Swan	E F												
Tundra Swan	F												
Wood Duck	F												
Gadwall	F G												
Eurasian Wigeon	F M												
American Wigeon	F M												
American Black Duck	D E F G H												
Mallard	E F G H M N												
Blue-winged Teal	F												
Northern Shoveler	F												
Northern Pintail	F G												
Green-winged Teal	F E												
Canvasback	E F												
Redhead	F												
Ring-necked Duck	F												
Greater Scaup	E F												
Lesser Scaup	F												
King Eider	A D E												
Common Eider	A B D E P												
Harlequin Duck	A D												
Surf Scoter	A B D E P												

COMMON NAMES	HABITAT	JAN	FEB	MAR	APR	MAY	JUN	JUL	AUG	SEP	OCT	NOV	DEC
White-winged Scoter	A B D E P												
Black Scoter	A B D E P												
Long-tailed Duck	A B E												
Bufflehead	A B E F												
Common Goldeneye	A B E F												
Barrow's Goldeneye	E												
Hooded Merganser	F G												
Common Merganser	A B E F												
Red-breasted Merganser	A B E P S												
Ruddy Duck	F												
Ring-necked Pheasant	L M N												
Northern Bobwhite	L M N												
Guinea Fowl	L M N												
Red-throated Loon	A B												
Common Loon	A B E												
Pied-billed Grebe	F G H												
Horned Grebe	B E												
Red-necked Grebe	B E												
Northern Fulmar	A												
Cory's Shearwater	A												
Greater Shearwater	A												
Sooty Shearwater	A												
Manx Shearwater	A												
Wilson's Storm-Petrel	A P												

55

COMMON NAMES	HABITAT	JAN	FEB	MAR	APR	MAY	JUN	JUL	AUG	SEP	OCT	NOV	DEC
Leach's Storm-Petrel	A P												
Northern Gannet	A P												
Double-crested Cormorant	D F												
Great Cormorant	D F												
American Bittern	G H I												
Great Blue Heron	C G H												
Great Egret	G H												
Snowy Egret	C G H												
Little Blue Heron	C G H												
Tricolored Heron	C G H												
Cattle Egret	M												
Green Heron	C G H												
Black-crowned Night-Heron	D C G H												
Yellow-crowned Night-Heron	C G H												
Glossy Ibis	G H I												
Black Vulture	M												
Turkey Vulture	M												
Osprey	F												
Bald Eagle	M												
Swallow-tailed Kite	I L M												
Northern Harrier	G H I M												
Sharp-shinned Hawk	M N												
Cooper's Hawk	J M												
Northern Goshawk	J K												

56

COMMON NAMES	HABITAT	JAN	FEB	MAR	APR	MAY	JUN	JUL	AUG	SEP	OCT	NOV	DEC
Red-shouldered Hawk	K M												
Broad-winged Hawk	M												
Red-tailed Hawk	J K M												
Rough-legged Hawk	M												
Clapper Rail	G												
Virginia Rail	G H												
Sora	G H												
Common Moorhen	F G												
American Coot	F												
Sandhill Crane	M												
Black-bellied Plover	B C G M S												
American Golden-Plover	M C												
Semipalmated Plover	B C G H												
Piping Plover	B C												
Killdeer	M												
American Oystercatcher	B G S												
Black-necked Stilt	C F G												
Greater Yellowlegs	C G												
Lesser Yellowlegs	C G												
Solitary Sandpiper	G H I												
Willet	C G												
Spotted Sandpiper	C F G H												
Upland Sandpiper	M												
Whimbrel	C G												

57

COMMON NAMES	HABITAT	JAN	FEB	MAR	APR	MAY	JUN	JUL	AUG	SEP	OCT	NOV	DEC
Hudsonian Godwit	C G M												
Marbled Godwit	B C G												
Ruddy Turnstone	C D S												
Red Knot	C G S												
Sanderling	B C G S												
Semipalmated Sandpiper	B C F G												
Western Sandpiper	C F G												
Least Sandpiper	C F G												
White-rumped Sandpiper	C F G												
Baird's Sandpiper	C F												
Pectoral Sandpiper	C G I M												
Purple Sandpiper	D												
Dunlin	B C G												
Stilt Sandpiper	C F G												
Buff-breasted Sandpiper	B M												
Ruff	C G												
Short-billed Dowitcher	C G												
Common Snipe	H I												
American Woodcock	H M												
Wilson's Phalarope	C G												
Red-necked Phalarope	A B E												
Red Phalarope	A B E												
Pomarine Jaeger	A B D												
Parasitic Jaeger	A B D												

COMMON NAMES	HABITAT	JAN	FEB	MAR	APR	MAY	JUN	JUL	AUG	SEP	OCT	NOV	DEC
Dovekie	A B E P	•	•	•	•							•	•
Common Murre	A B	•	•	•									•
Thick-billed Murre	A B	•	•	•	•							•	•
Razorbill	A B P	•	•	•								•	•
Black Guillemot	A B	•	•	•	•	•	•	•	•	•	•	•	•
Atlantic Puffin	A B P	•	•	•	•	•	•	•	•	•	•	•	•
Laughing Gull	B C G S	•			•	•	•	•	•	•	•		•
Little Gull	B	•	•	•	•								•
Black-headed Gull	B E G	•	•	•	•								•
Bonaparte's Gull	A B E	•	•						•	•	•	•	•
Ring-billed Gull	B C E F G	•	•	•	•	•	•	•	•	•	•	•	•
Herring Gull	ABCDEFGS	•	•	•	•	•	•	•	•	•	•	•	•
Iceland Gull	B	•	•	•	•	•	•						•
Lesser Black-backed Gull	B C D E	•	•	•	•								•
Glaucous Gull	B	•	•	•	•								•
Great Black-backed Gull	ABCDEFGS	•	•	•	•	•	•	•	•	•	•	•	•
Sabine's Gull	B D E									•	•		
Black-legged Kittiwake	A	•	•	•	•	•					•	•	•
Caspian Tern	B C G						•	•	•	•			
Royal Tern	B C G						•	•	•	•		•	
Sandwich Tern	B C D E S						•	•	•	•			
Roseate Tern	B C D E F S					•	•	•	•	•	•		
Common Tern	B C D E S					•	•	•	•	•	•		•
Arctic Tern	C G					•	•	•	•	•	•		

COMMON NAMES	HABITAT	JAN	FEB	MAR	APR	MAY	JUN	JUL	AUG	SEP	OCT	NOV	DEC
Forster's Tern	B E C												
Least Tern	B C D												
Sooty Tern	B C D												
Black Tern	B E G												
Black Skimmer	B C E G												
Rock Pigeon	N												
White-winged Dove	N												
Mourning Dove	J K M N												
Black-billed Cuckoo	J K L M												
Yellow-billed Cuckoo	J K N												
Barn Owl	K												
Snowy Owl	B M O												
Long-eared Owl	K												
Short-eared Owl	M O												
Northern Saw-whet Owl	K												
Common Nighthawk	H N												
Whip-poor-will	J												
Chimney Swift	N												
Ruby-throated Hummingbird	N												
Belted Kingfisher	E F G												
Red-headed Woodpecker	K J M N												
Red-bellied Woodpecker	K N												
Yellow-bellied Sapsucker	J K												
Downy Woodpecker	J K N												

COMMON NAMES	HABITAT	JAN	FEB	MAR	APR	MAY	JUN	JUL	AUG	SEP	OCT	NOV	DEC
Hairy Woodpecker	K N												
Northern Flicker	K M N												
American Kestrel	M												
Merlin	C K M												
Peregrine Falcon	G K M												
Olive-sided Flycatcher	J K												
Eastern Wood-Pewee	K												
Yellow-bellied Flycatcher	J K L												
Alder Flycatcher	J K L												
Willow Flycatcher	J K L												
Least Flycatcher	K												
Eastern Phoebe	K L N												
Great Crested Flycatcher	J K												
Western Kingbird	M												
Eastern Kingbird	M												
Scissor-tailed Flycatcher	I L M												
Northern Shrike	L M												
White-eyed Vireo	H K												
Yellow-throated Vireo	H J K												
Blue-headed Vireo	J K												
Warbling Vireo	J K N												
Philadelphia Vireo	J K												
Red-eyed Vireo	J K												
Blue Jay	J K N												

COMMON NAMES	HABITAT	JAN	FEB	MAR	APR	MAY	JUN	JUL	AUG	SEP	OCT	NOV	DEC
American Crow	J K L M												
Horned Lark	M O												
Purple Martin	F M N												
Tree Swallow	F H M												
Northern Rough-winged Swallow	F H												
Bank Swallow	B F H												
Cliff Swallow	F H												
Barn Swallow	E F G H M												
Black-capped Chickadee	J K N												
Red-breasted Nuthatch	J K N												
White-breasted Nuthatch	J K N												
Brown Creeper	J K N												
Carolina Wren	H N												
House Wren	N												
Winter Wren	K N												
Sedge Wren	H												
Marsh Wren	H												
Golden-crowned Kinglet	K N												
Ruby-crowned Kinglet	K N												
Blue-gray Gnatcatcher	J K N												
Northern Wheatear	M O												
Eastern Bluebird	M N												
Veery	K												
Gray-cheeked Thrush	K												

62

COMMON NAMES	HABITAT	JAN	FEB	MAR	APR	MAY	JUN	JUL	AUG	SEP	OCT	NOV	DEC
Swainson's Thrush	K												
Hermit Thrush	K												
Wood Thrush	J K N												
American Robin	J K L M N												
Gray Catbird	L N												
Northern Mockingbird	N												
Brown Thrasher	L M N												
European Starling	J K L M N												
American Pipit	M												
Bohemian Waxwing	J K N												
Cedar Waxwing	J K N												
Lapland Longspur	G O												
Snow Bunting	B M O												
Blue-winged Warbler	J K N												
Golden-winged Warbler	J K N												
Tennessee Warbler	J K N												
Orange-crowned Warbler	K L												
Nashville Warbler	J K N												
Northern Parula	K N												
Yellow Warbler	J K L N												
Chestnut-sided Warbler	J K N												
Magnolia Warbler	J K L N												
Cape May Warbler	J K L N												
Black-throated Blue Warbler	J K L N												

COMMON NAMES	HABITAT	JAN	FEB	MAR	APR	MAY	JUN	JUL	AUG	SEP	OCT	NOV	DEC
Yellow-rumped Warbler	J K L M N												
Black-throated Green Warbler	J K L N												
Blackburnian Warbler	J K N												
Yellow-throated Warbler	J K N												
Pine Warbler	K												
Prairie Warbler	K L N												
Palm Warbler	K N O												
Bay-breasted Warbler	J K N												
Blackpoll Warbler	J K N												
Cerulean Warbler	J K N												
Black-and-white Warbler	J K N												
American Redstart	J K N												
Prothonotary Warbler	J K N												
Worm-eating Warbler	J K												
Ovenbird	J K												
Northern Waterthrush	H J K												
Louisiana Waterthrush	H												
Kentucky Warbler	J K N												
Connecticut Warbler	J K N												
Mourning Warbler	J K N												
Common Yellowthroat	K L M N												
Hooded Warbler	J K N												
Wilson's Warbler	J K N												
Canada Warbler	J K N												

COMMON NAMES	HABITAT	JAN	FEB	MAR	APR	MAY	JUN	JUL	AUG	SEP	OCT	NOV	DEC
Yellow-breasted Chat	J K N O												
Summer Tanager	J K N												
Scarlet Tanager	J K N												
Western Tanager	J K N												
Eastern Towhee	K L												
American Tree Sparrow	L M N												
Chipping Sparrow	M N												
Clay-colored Sparrow	K M N												
Field Sparrow	M N												
Vesper Sparrow	M O												
Lark Sparrow	M												
Savannah Sparrow	G M O												
Grasshopper Sparrow	M												
Saltmarsh Sparrow	G												
Fox Sparrow	M N												
Song Sparrow	J K L M N												
Lincoln's Sparrow	H K L												
Swamp Sparrow	H M												
White-throated Sparrow	J K M N												
White-crowned Sparrow	M N												
Dark-eyed Junco	K M N												
Northern Cardinal	N												
Rose-breasted Grosbeak	J K N												
Blue Grosbeak	M N												

65

COMMON NAMES	HABITAT	JAN	FEB	MAR	APR	MAY	JUN	JUL	AUG	SEP	OCT	NOV	DEC
Indigo Bunting	M N												
Dickcissel	N												
Bobolink	J K N												
Red-winged Blackbird	M N												
Eastern Meadowlark	M												
Yellow-headed Blackbird	M N												
Rusty Blackbird	H J												
Common Grackle	K M N												
Brown-headed Cowbird	M N												
Orchard Oriole	J N												
Baltimore Oriole	J K N												
Pine Grosbeak	K N												
Purple Finch	N												
House Finch	N												
Red Crossbill	K												
White-winged Crossbill	K												
Common Redpoll	N O												
Pine Siskin	K N O												
American Goldfinch	M N												
Evening Grosbeak	J K N												
House Sparrow	M N												

Selected References

American Birding Association. 1994. *A Birder's Guide to Eastern Massachusetts.* American Birding Association, Colorado Springs, CO.

Bailey, Wallace. 1955. *Birds in Massachusetts.* The College Press, South Lancaster, MA.

Bailey, Wallace. 1968. *Birds of the Cape Cod National Seashore and Adjacent Areas.* Eastern National Park and Monument Association in cooperation with Cape Cod National Seashore, National Park Service, U.S. Department of the Interior, Washington, DC.

Bent, Arthur Cleveland 1961, *Life Histories of North American Birds*, Dover Publications, New York, NY.

Blodget, Bradford G. 1983. *List of the Birds of Massachusetts* (3rd Edition). Massachusetts Division of Fisheries, Boston, MA.

Dunn, Jon L. and Jonathan Alderfer (Editors). 2011. *Field Guide to the Birds of North America, Sixth Edition.* National Geographic Society, Washington, DC.

Forbush, Edward Howe. 1927. *Birds of Massachusetts and Other New England States.* Three Volumes. Commonwealth of Massachusetts, Boston, MA.

Griscom, Ludlow and Dorothy E. Snyder. 1955. *The Birds of Massachusetts.* The Anthoensen Press, Portland, ME.

Griscom, Ludlow and Edith Folger. 1948. *The Birds of Nantucket.* Harvard University Press, Cambridge, MA.

Hill, Norman, P. 1965. *The Birds of Cape Cod, Massachusetts.* William Morrow and Co., New York, NY.

Kaufman, Kenn, 2000, *Kaufman Field Guide to Birds of North America,* Houghton Mifflin, New York, NY.

Massachusetts Audubon Society. 1998. *A Checklist of the Birds of Massachusetts.* Massachusetts Audubon Society, Lincoln, MA

Petersen, Wayne R. and Roger Meservey. 2003. *Massachusetts Breeding Bird Atlas.* University of Massachusetts Press, Amherst, MA

Peterson, Roger Tory. 2002. *Birds of Eastern and Central North America, Fifth Edition.* Peterson Field Guide Series, Houghton Mifflin Co., New York, NY.

Sibley, David Allen. 2014. *The Sibley Guide to Birds, Second Edition.* Alfred A. Knopf, New York, NY.

Veit, Richard R. and Wayne R. Petersen. 1993. *Birds of Massachusetts.* Massachusetts Audubon Society, Lincoln MA.

59961450R00040

Made in the USA
Middletown, DE
13 August 2019